Voysey's Birds and Animals

Voysey's Birds and Animals

Karen Livingstone

Thames & Hudson | V&A

Contents

Preface

The architect and designer Charles Francis Annesley Voysey (1857–1941) was renowned for his innovative architecture and his invention of a new language in decorative design based on animal and bird life.

Voysey was a central and influential figure of the Arts and Crafts Movement, a design reform movement that was at its height in Britain from around 1880. As an architect and prolific designer of domestic furnishings Voysey had an instantly recognizable style, which he established early in his career and applied consistently across all his work with great variety and imagination. In his pattern designs for textiles and wallpaper he introduced bold flattening of motifs, fresh new colours and unusual combinations. He created signature motifs, including hearts, birds and animals, in a way that was innovative and radical. Like many Arts and Crafts designers, Voysey drew his inspiration from a direct study of nature, yet he remained uniquely individual – an 'inventor' – in the way he translated nature into his designs. His designs were popular and much imitated at the time but also, at first, maligned and mistrusted.

The selection of designs featured in the book is drawn from the collections of the Victoria and Albert Museum. The museum holds more than five hundred of Voysey's designs, examples of wallpapers and furnishing fabrics. It began collecting his designs during his lifetime: as early as 1913 he was asked to donate some examples of his work. This donation was supplemented by further gifts and acquisitions, from both Voysey and the manufacturers who produced his wallpapers and fabrics. A small selection of Voysey's sketches and designs from the archives of the Royal Institute of British Architects (RIBA), London, is also included.

This book reveals the full, delightful range of birds and animals that form the central motifs and character of Voysey's designs for wallpaper and textiles, and explains the ideas and symbolism that lay behind them. The designs confirm the full range of Voysey's creativity and inventiveness, and the enduring appeal of his work to this day.

Fig. 1 Detail from design for a textile, 1919 (pp. 102–3)

Introduction

'The life of animals might be a source of joy in our own lives'

Charles Francis Annesley Voysey was acclaimed for his architecture and his mastery of design in many media. He was skilled in drawing, lettering and graphic design, and was a successful and prolific designer of patterns for furnishing fabrics and wallpapers, and of furniture, clocks, jewellery, stained glass, ceramics, sculpture and metalwork. His reputation was secured in Britain and internationally through the widespread exhibition and publication of all his design work and of his writing and lectures.

As a central figure of the Arts and Crafts Movement in Britain, Voysey believed in living a simple, honest and homely life, lived close to nature. Arts and Crafts was an ideas-driven movement, which informally bound a diverse range of people and products through a shared concern about the impact of industrialization on social conditions and traditional craftsmanship. It was also a reaction against the inventive, but over-elaborate and thoughtless, design of the Victorian mechanized age. Voysey did not share the socialist beliefs of other leaders of the movement such as William Morris (1834–1896) and C.R. Ashbee (1863–1942), but he was concerned with the economics of architecture and design, wanting them to be affordable. He believed himself to be an architect and designer in the tradition of the Gothic revival, reinventing old forms and designing not only buildings but also everything that went in them.

Voysey (fig. 2) was once described as a 'solemn, frail, bird-like, man, whose most remarkable attribute was said to be his lovely smile, full of kindness, humour and affection'.[1] The clue

Fig. 2 Photograph of C.F.A. Voysey, taken at an exhibition of his work at the Batsford Gallery, London, in 1931 Published on the cover of *The Architect and Building News*, London, 21 February 1941 Victoria and Albert Museum: National Art Library (38041800873382)

The
ARCHITECT
and Building News

February 21, 1941

THE LATE C. F. A. VOYSEY

We very much regret to announce the death last week of Mr. Charles Annesley Voysey. An obituary appears on the next page.

Fig. 3 A device symbolizing a spiritual
and wise messenger, designed by
Voysey for the frontispiece of his
book *Individuality*, published in 1915
Ink on paper
Crab Tree Farm

INTRODUCTION

to the solemn element of Voysey's character lay in his religious faith, which informed his belief that a higher purpose could be achieved through art and design. He was interested in designing beautiful things as a way of improving everyday life and contributing to society.

Symbolism played an important role in his approach, and he deliberately selected motifs, such as animals, birds, hearts and angels, to create designs which expressed his beliefs and values. This approach is encapsulated in the device he designed as the frontispiece for *Individuality* (fig. 3), an essay published in 1915 in which Voysey made links between inner creativity and spirituality and called for the celebration of the individual over collectivism. He later explained that the device:

> is intended to suggest that all life is anointed by the spirit. The angel, therefore, as spiritual messenger, is watering the oak, which latter is the symbol of hearty growth; we speak of hearts of oak, and so this one is sustained by the heart of man which denotes the affections, and supports likewise the raven as a symbol of animal life. Birds, like men, walk erect, and they also soar into the sky and so symbolise aspiration and spiritual activity. The raven is here chosen for its supposed wonderful sagacity. Although it has been stated that the eagle is the highest flyer and the furthest seer of any living creature.[2]

Voysey believed that nature was the 'fountain-head', or source, of all design, and also that it had a strong moral dimension. However, while symbolism and faith informed everything Voysey did, the customer did not have to understand the meaning behind his designs. The principal outcome was to provide beautiful, simple design for the home, fit for the purpose and for the place and time.

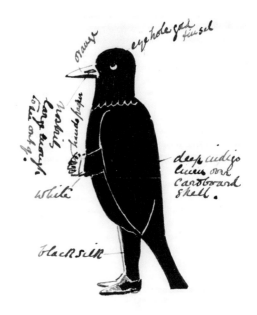

Fig. 4 Design by Voysey for a blackbird
fancy-dress costume, undated
Ink on paper
Private Collection

Fig. 5 *Four and Twenty Blackbirds*,
design for a wallpaper for
Sanderson & Co., 1908
Ink washes on tracing paper
Royal Institute of British Architects
(RIBA: S8119/VOY[858])

Portraiture, caricature, popular rhymes and mottos greatly interested Voysey. He had a good sense of humour and a talent for capturing a likeness – whether of people, or of animals and birds, or a combination of both. The more serious side of his personality and his use of symbolism were counterbalanced by his sense of fun and active participation in the guilds, societies, committees, clubs, parties and social events of the Arts and Crafts Movement. His design for a fancy-dress costume, probably for a ball at one of the clubs he belonged to,[3] was, true to spirit, a blackbird, complete with orange beak and nostrils large enough to see through (fig. 4). Voysey also designed a series of posters and wallpapers that drew on popular sayings or nursery rhymes and featured animals and birds, including *Hey Diddle Diddle* for

Essex & Co. in 1904[4] and *Four and Twenty Blackbirds* (fig. 5) for Sandersons in 1908.

Voysey introduced an inventive and radical approach to using motifs based on animals and birds by stylizing them and distilling them to pure, flat forms. In this way he created a new style and decorative language that was much admired and imitated and advanced the genre of pattern design and production.

Others before him, such as William Morris, had broken from the design and production techniques of the recent past by creating patterns dense with beautiful renderings of birds, animals and flowers inspired by the Middle Ages. Voysey took a different approach, abstracting the same birds, animals and flowers into stylized flat motifs and spacious patterns, eliminating all but the essential detail and inspired by what he could see and study around him.

Voysey's use of colour was also innovative, as he and his contemporaries moved deliberately away from the vivid chemical dyes and muddy colour schemes that reflected earlier Victorian tastes to new, more natural dyes and colours. He worked with light, clear colour combinations to 'raise the colour sense from morbid sickly despondency to bright and hopeful cheeriness. Crudity, if you will, rather than mud and mourning.'[5] This was much more suited to his favoured subject matter of nature and the wildlife of the British countryside.

His application of colour in flat washes and even tones, with a limited colour palette, sometimes outlined in white or black lines to create a sense of space, contributed to his creation of a new style and helped establish him as one of the most influential designers of his age.

Organizations such as the Arts and Crafts Exhibition Society (founded in London in 1887) helped to promote the work of Voysey and his contemporaries though their exhibitions. British designers became well known internationally through the new art journals being published across Europe and America. Notable among these was *The Studio*, which featured its first interview with Voysey in 1893 and from then on regularly published photographs of his architecture and designs. He became adept at ensuring that his work was displayed in these magazines, helping to secure his reputation and influence – so much so that by 1896 *The Studio* was reporting that a 'Voysey wallpaper' was as familiar as a 'Morris chintz' or a 'Liberty silk'.[6] By 1900 his style was so recognizable that a commentator in *The Studio* wrote that 'To the public at large Mr Voysey is perhaps best known by his characteristic designs for wallpapers and textiles. His unzoological birds and fantastic foliage are truly inimitable.'[7] This popularity led to many inferior imitations.

At first, however, some manufacturers were reluctant to take a chance with his designs, and commercial success was not always guaranteed. In 1909 Voysey railed against those who thought his designs featuring stylized patterns based on animal and bird life could not be commercially successful, setting out his view that:

> The use of animal life is dependent on our spiritual activity. If we are thoroughly materialistic, we prefer fruit and flowers in our wall-papers and fabrics, and feel hurt by the mutilation of birds or animals when cut round furniture or upholstered on to seats. But if the rendering of our animals in decoration is so conventional that we feel only the spirit of the beast is recorded, no pain is felt. The martlet in heraldry never pained anyone, but a very realistic bird with all its feathers carefully drawn and its legs cut off would pain us at once, the dominant impression or idea being, a very material bird injured, mutilated, and maimed. While, in the case of the martlet, the illustration is of the bird spirit; it is a generic bird, not any particular species.[8]

Despite some objections to his designs, Voysey was a prolific and innovative designer, who as late as the 1920s was still being named as the 'Genius of Pattern' in advertisements for the wallpaper manufacturer Essex & Co. By 1931, at a retrospective exhibition of his work at the Batsford Gallery in London, the final impression for one critic was the enduring strength of Voysey's convictions. He found that:

> the proof lies in the unbroken unity of his design in every medium. Ornament indeed has never been to his mind; his inborn puritanism spurns it. Rather he has striven to get down to bones and structure and bend

them to his purposes. The Voysey Bird is proverbial, and hops gaily about the walls of the Batsford Gallery; but flowers too, shrubs, trees, lions, seahorses must all be trained to the style of the Flora et Fauna Voyseyana before he will have any truck with them.[9]

Background and Influences

Voysey belonged to the generation of radical and reforming architects and designers who followed in the footsteps of the critic and author John Ruskin (1819–1900) and the designer, writer and social activist William Morris to form the Arts and Crafts Movement in Britain.

Voysey acknowledged the influence of the generation of architects and designers of the Gothic Revival who came before him, especially A.W.N. Pugin (1812–1852), George Edmund Street (1824–1881) and Richard Norman Shaw (1831–1912). These were architects who not only designed great buildings, but also their interiors, including wallpaper, textiles, tiles, furniture and metalwork.

Pugin was an especially important influence. He also formed a link for Voysey between religion and his chosen profession of architecture. Pugin held strong moral and religious beliefs, as did Voysey, whose father was an infamous and controversial minister. The wallpapers Pugin designed for his own home, The Grange, Ramsgate, and for the interiors of the Palace of Westminster, London, were an important precedent for Voysey's pattern design, in the use of birds as motifs[10] and especially in the flattening of form to reflect the flat surface of the wall (fig. 6).

Like Pugin, the design reformers of the mid-nineteenth century, Owen Jones (1809–1874) and Christopher Dresser (1834–1904), advocated direct study from nature. Publications such as Owen Jones's *Grammar of Ornament* (1856) proposed

Fig. 6 *The Syracuse*, portion of wallpaper, designed by Voysey and manufactured by Essex & Co., London, 1902–3
Colour woodblock print on paper
Victoria and Albert Museum, London
(V&A: E.470-1967)

INTRODUCTION

the abstraction, flattening and repetition of motifs, new colour combinations, the use of positive and negative areas, and applying the 'machine-age principle of clarity and simplicity'[11] to pattern design. These were all characteristics which Voysey adopted into his designs and then made his own.

Voysey first learned the technicalities of drawing repeating patterns in 1883 from his friend and fellow designer A.H. Mackmurdo (1851–1942), who he said 'impressed him even more than Morris'.[12] In 1882 Mackmurdo had established a society, the Century Guild with Selwyn Image (1849–1930), and they designed distinctive and original wallpaper patterns

Fig. 7 Design for a tile, *c*.1900
Watercolour on paper
Crab Tree Farm

for forward-looking firms such as Jeffrey & Co. Voysey's earl-iest pattern designs show the influence of Mackmurdo's style, including the use of 'fresher lighter forms ... than Morris',[13] the whiplash curves of snakes and dragons and the sense of movement in the flocks of birds in flight that was to become one of Voysey's hallmarks.

Voysey also acknowledged that one of the greatest influences on him was William Morris, yet he remained cautious and disci-plined in what he was prepared to glean from Morris's example. Memorably, he recalled standing as a young man outside the newly opened Morris & Co. shop on London's Oxford Street, unwilling and afraid to go inside in case he was overawed and corrupted by what he saw.[14]

In his designs, William Morris emphasized the beautiful and naturalistic rendering of birds, animals and flowers, and drew inspiration from the medieval past. Voysey, in contrast, took these forms directly from the natural world he could see all around him and distilled them into flat, stylized, repeating motifs. Voysey also designed with primary emphasis on the effect of the pattern, saying in an interview in 1893 that 'A wallpaper should always be essentially a pattern, the repeat of which is one of the main characteristics, rather than a pattern disguising a repeat.'[15] Comparing this approach to how Morris handled pattern, one later commentator observed that 'Voysey characteristically conceives a design as a pattern and seeks to emphasize the pattern; with Morris the pattern is never emphasized, but appears rather as a restriction imposed by the need for repetition.'[16]

When Voysey began selling his first designs in the late 1880s[17] he could not perhaps have imagined that they would become so popular that he would later be under contract to produce patterns for all the major manufacturers of artistic textiles and wallpaper, nor that they would be sold and exhibited in the fashionable spaces of London and as far afield as Antwerp, Brussels, Helsinki and Paris. He began designing patterns originally to help support his young family while he built up his architecture practice, which he had founded in 1882. Selling pattern designs would remain a vital, although limited, source of income later in his life, after his practice folded and he was living alone and again struggling financially.

Voysey was a prolific and fast producer of patterns, and was keen to sell his work without specifying whether the designs should be used for wallpaper, printed or woven textiles, or even tile panels (fig. 7). The same designs, or variations on the same themes, were in fact picked up by different manufacturers.

Fig. 8 *The Pelican in her Piety*,
carved in plasticine by Voysey
and possibly cast at Hollinshead
& Burton Foundry, Thames
Ditton, Surrey, 1920
Bronze
Crab Tree Farm

Stylistically, the designs he produced between 1890 and 1900 were perhaps his most confident and abstracted. After 1900 he adopted a lighter touch and created patterns made up of a few individual motifs simply drawn, limited in the number of colours and arranged together with plenty of space around them.

Voysey himself was not a great advocate of using patterned wallpapers and fabrics in the home, preferring the option of wood panelling or plain colour rather than pattern. However, wallpaper was the more economic choice, and in fact he did use wallpaper of his own design to decorate his home, because it was affordable within his limited budget. For his home The Orchard in Chorleywood, for example, he selected the wallpaper *The Squire's Garden* (plate 45), a pattern of peacocks, to decorate

Fig. 9 Photograph of furniture and
furnishings designed by Voysey
Published in *Dekorative Kunst,*
vol. 1, no. 6 (March 1898)
Victoria and Albert Museum:
National Art Library (38041800873341)

the Play and Schoolroom, but otherwise most of the rooms were painted a single plain colour.

The body of work illustrated in this book focuses on Voysey's pattern designs for textiles and wallpapers, but he applied the same principles of simplicity to his designs for furniture, jewellery, metalwork, stained glass and other materials. On the occasions when he did apply decoration, he consistently applied his design language and the use of symbols and motifs based on nature, and in particular birds (fig. 8).

One of Voysey's earliest and more unusual pieces of furniture was an armchair which came to be known as the 'swan' chair after the birds' heads carved on the uprights.[18] A variation on this chair type was published in 1898 (fig. 9) and also appears to

Fig. 10 Ventilator grille,
designed by Voysey and probably
manufactured by Comyn,
Ching & Co., Ipswich,
Suffolk, c.1892
Cast iron
Victoria and Albert Museum, London
(V&A: M.70-2014)

have birds' heads terminating the arms. Carved or inlaid decoration on Voysey's furniture was quite rare and always restrained, but he did occasionally add small bird sculptures to a sideboard or bed, for example, incorporating them for their symbolic properties. As he explained:

> You shall perch four eagles on my bedposts to drive away bad spirits, as the Byzantines believed, and rest my fire-irons on the backs of brass cats, not dogs, for cats are the most faithful fireside dwellers. On my table let there be fruit and flowers and one or two symbolic animals, and let the foods be handed round.[19]

In the same 1898 photograph as the swan chair, there is a 'lady's work cabinet' with a large pierced brass hinge decorated with birds. Voysey's decorative metalwork hinges, ventilation grilles (fig. 10), fire screens and sculptures all featured his signature symbol of a bird (fig. 11). Some fire tongs and accessories exhibited and published in 1903 were topped with 'His own decorative symbol ... a bird of wise Egyptian countenance which appears very cunningly perched on the bulbs which end the uprights of a brass firescreen.'[20]

Fig. 11 Photograph taken in 1900 of a group of bronze sculptures, pen tray and ink well designed by Voysey Royal Institute of British Architects (RIBA: Br Jo/Box 7/20)

Nature and Inspiration
Voysey, like many Arts and Crafts designers, sought inspiration directly from nature, believing it was important to observe nature

INTRODUCTION

directly – as did the enameller and jeweller Henry Wilson, who instructed someone making a pendant depicting a nightingale to 'first, go and watch one singing'.[21] Voysey further believed that 'ideas were influenced and stimulated by the thoughts and feelings in the things around them'.[22] During his life he moved between London and the countryside, but even when he moved permanently to London it was the world of animals, birds and nature that he consistently chose as the subject of his designs (figs. 12, 13).

Between the ages of 7 and 14, Voysey lived among the fields and farmland of North Yorkshire, in the rural parish of Healaugh, 'a remote country parish, three miles from the nearest town, four miles from the nearest station, three miles from a doctor'.[23] His infant years had been spent moving between the East Riding

Fig. 12 Writing desk, designed by Voysey and possibly made by F.C. Nielsen, London, 1895
Oak with copper hinges
Victoria and Albert Museum, London
(V&A: W.6-1953)

Fig. 13 Design for a writing desk, 1895
Pencil, ink and watercolour on paper
Victoria and Albert Museum, London
(V&A: E.274-1913)

INTRODUCTION

of Yorkshire, Jamaica and east London, following the path of his father's tempestuous career. Once the family had settled again in Yorkshire no formal education was available to Voysey, and he passed much of his time in the company of his father, visiting parishioners on the 'peasant' farms and helping his father, a 'keen gardener', tend to their 'large garden and orchards'.[24] Perhaps it was during these years that he developed his skills in observing nature, and his knowledge and love of native flowers and farm animals.

In 1871, when Voysey was 14, the family moved back to London. Unhappy at his new school, Dulwich College, Voysey would perhaps have found solace walking in nearby Dulwich Woods. We do not know if the young Voysey adopted a habit of drawing and sketching from nature in these formative years, but by the time he left school at the age of 17 and became an apprenticed architect, he had an evident talent for drawing, even though he had been strongly discouraged in this area by his school art master.

From then on Voysey lived mostly in urban surroundings, in various parts of London including Streatham and St John's Wood, and he gradually became part of the metropolitan life and infrastructure of the artistic circles of the Arts and Crafts Movement. Most of the houses he built for his clients were in rural settings, in the Lake District (reached by train) or Surrey. To reach the sites of his buildings close to London, Voysey would set off early in the morning on his bicycle, no doubt enjoying the countryside and observing its bird and animal life on the way.

Voysey ran his studio from home, and on his desk was a small stationery cabinet decorated with beaten metal hinges featuring a pair of his signature birds (fig. 14). He also had peacock feathers on display on his desk and around his home. Peacocks have been used symbolically in many contexts throughout history, and were a favoured Arts and Crafts motif. Voysey chose the peacock motif as the device that represented the values of protection, integrity

Fig. 14 Photograph of Voysey's desk in his study at 6 Carlton Hill, London, published in *The Studio*, vol. 7 (1896), p. 215 Victoria and Albert Museum: National Art Library (38041800872988)

INTRODUCTION

ELIZABETH H & ANNESLEY ✠ VOYSEY ✠ PHYLLIS ·

28   INTRODUCTION

and longevity. The bookplates he designed for his children also included birds or animals as their main symbols. The design for his son Annesley and daughter-in-law Phyllis includes an owl (representing wisdom), a squirrel, a dove (love) in an olive tree (peace), and a rabbit, among flowers on a grassy mound (nature) (fig. 15).

For a few golden years during his adult life, Voysey lived surrounded by the nature that inspired him, in the house he designed in 1899, The Orchard in Chorleywood, a suitable location for his young family north-west of London. Constrained by his limited finances, Voysey — always concerned with the economics of house-building — made every choice about the detailing and finish of The Orchard himself, in accordance with his budget. The Orchard was his ideal, affordable small home.

Voysey was not materially driven, and wanted just enough money to live on and support his family. Unfortunately the combination of a declining architectural practice, as fashion and the economy changed in the early twentieth century, and an increasingly difficult home life (he and his wife, Mary Maria, were to divorce in 1917), contributed to the Voyseys' decision to sell The Orchard in 1906. The family then moved to a rented home in Hampstead, north London, close to Voysey's father and the progressive King Alfred's School, which the children attended.

Voysey's architectural career, and his reputation at home and abroad, were at their peak around the time that he designed The Orchard (fig. 16). Photographs of it were widely published, and in an article Voysey described its design and qualities fondly, especially noting that

From the south window Chorley Wood Common is to be seen over trees, high hedges, and ditches in the valley between, and not a house or building of any kind will ever rise to mar the view. Nightingales, larks, linnets,

Fig. 15 Bookplate designed by Voysey for his son and daughter-in-law, 1923
Ink on paper
Crab Tree Farm

thrushes, blackbirds, wood pigeons, and even foxes,
deign to keep company with the little white house.[25]

This description leads us straight into Voysey's designs. They
feature a wide variety of birds and animals, ranging from accurate
depictions to abstracted motifs deployed as repeating patterns.
It is possible to identify many of the species of animals and birds
in his designs, while others are likenesses that have been distilled
or abstracted for decorative effect, although leaving no doubt that
their origins lay in studying from life.

INTRODUCTION

Voysey's working sketches and notes reveal that drawing from nature was an important part of his method for making designs, with birds and animals as the central motifs (see 4, 8 and 10). He collected pages from magazines with illustrations of animals and birds and sketched from reference books such as Richard Lydekker's *The Royal Natural History* (1896). He also made numerous sketches of birds and animals, annotated with notes about colour and character, on visits to London Zoo, the Natural History Museum, and London's parks. His account book records expenses for trips to the zoo to study eagles,[26] and he wrote about his observations and feelings on these visits:

> When we contemplate the eagle, even in captivity, in the Zoological Gardens, how can we resist a feeling, a reverent admiration for his superb dignity, and contemplative grandeur. Not only for his far sight, but for his nobility, is the eagle the aristocrat of birds, and their premier peer. As we look up to the noble and the Godlike, so also, we aspire.[27]

Back in his studio, Voysey worked quickly and inventively, refining his sketches and distilling his drawings of birds and animals to just a few simple lines and shapes. Many of the species he incorporated into his designs are identifiable because of his initial detailed study, and his skill in capturing likeness and expression with just a few strokes and suggestions of colour (fig. 17).

Birds

Voysey used birds in his designs with an inventiveness, frequency and variety unmatched by any other Arts and Crafts designer. His early designs (from the period 1884–90) on which he initially established his popularity and reputation were predominantly based on floral and plant motifs. Birds first featured in his designs from around 1891, but the motif was not welcomed instantly into the world of manufacturing and retail, as Voysey recalled in a speech in 1927:

> When architectural commissions were scarce, with characteristic courage Essex [the wallpaper manufacturer] ... dared to deal with my work. All his friends told him he was a fool to do so, but he persisted in spite of the fact that the public was opposed to birds and, in fact, everything that I did.[28]

In his landmark interview in *The Studio* in 1893, when Voysey was asked about his choice of birds as a decorative device, he replied:

> I do not see why the forms of birds ... may not be used, provided they are reduced to mere symbols. Decorators complain of small repeats and simple patterns, because they are apt to show the joints, and because the figures may be mutilated, in turning a corner, for instance. If the form be sufficiently conventionalised the mutilation is not felt; a real bird with his head cut off is an unpleasant sight, so is a rose that has lost half an inch of its petals; but if the bird is a crude symbol and his facsimile occurs complete within ten and a half inches' distance, although one may have lost a portion of his body, it does not violate my feelings. To go to Nature is of course, to approach the fountain-head, but a literal transcript will not result in good ornament; before a living plant a man must go through an elaborate process of selection and analysis, and think of the balance, repetition, and many other qualities of his design, thereby calling his individual taste into play and adding a human interest to his work. If he does this, although he has gone directly to Nature,

Fig. 17 *My Garden*, design for a textile or wallpaper, 1929 Watercolour and pencil on paper Victoria and Albert Museum, London (V&A: E.291-1974)

his work will not resemble any of his predecessors; he has become an inventor.[29]

The species depicted in the designs selected for this book include seagulls, owls, doves, canaries, eagles, herons, kingfishers, pelicans, peacocks, swallows, swans, ravens, crows, blackbirds and thrushes. These birds feature either singly, in pairs or in multiples, in flight or perched in trees and bushes. The quality they share is that they are all keenly observed and expertly drawn, to the extent that one commentator noted that:

> His birds, of which he makes use in large numbers and of many kinds, are remarkable for the identity of species. We can recognize them at once; and the few broad touches and washes by which they are represented usually show us some characteristic of the bird which we had not previously observed. Voysey's version of a particular kind of bird is more like the bird it depicts than the actual bird itself is.[30]

One of his most striking designs of all, *Birds of Many Climes* (1), brings together 15 species of birds from around the world. Birds from places as far apart as Australia, India, Ecuador, Colombia, South America and Japan are perched in a tree with flowers at its base. None of these would have co-existed except, perhaps, in the specimen cases of the Natural History Museum, London, but the design encapsulates much of Voysey's love of nature, and is an outstanding and joyful celebration of these 'things from the heavens [that] are nearer the spirit than the flesh'.[31]

Other Animals
Voysey's fascination with the natural world extended to a wonderful range of other animals and creatures, which allowed him to

show his 'delightful sense of humour', 'knack of fairy-tale telling' and his great strength in 'simplicity of expression'.[32] The animals he incorporated into his designs range from underwater snakes and sea creatures such as octopuses and seahorses, to prowling lions and tigers, kangaroos, monkeys and polar bears. They are treated either as naturalistic studies or as abstracted and strongly stylized designs, with motifs such as seahorses used on repeat.

Voysey's designs featuring snakes and dragons are limited to about four or five known examples. They demonstrate his early experimentation with strong lines and colour. The whip-lash style of these designs is associated with the development of the whiplash Art Nouveau style in Europe, from which Voysey strongly disassociated himself at the time, calling the style 'unhealthy and revolting'.[33] European Art Nouveau designers such as Hermann Obrist (1862–1927) and Henry Van de Velde (1863–1957) were great admirers of Voysey, but they perhaps owe more to the influence of his friend and teacher of pattern design A.H. Mackmurdo.

Voysey's skill in drawing and capturing the likeness of an animal can be seen in the series of small studies he made in pen and watercolour in 1927 (54, 55). Each of these creatures or plants had featured in some form in his earlier designs, and they are drawn with great character and lightness of touch, reflecting Voysey's enjoyment of nature and his lifetime of observing and drawing animal life with accuracy and love.

The animals with which Voysey is perhaps most closely associated, however, are the domestic, farm and forest animals that feature in his designs after 1900, including cows, sheep, cats, dogs, chickens, rabbits, squirrels and deer. Voysey's designs based on flattened and abstracted animals, like his bird designs, were considered to be both ingenious and pushing the boundaries of acceptable design (fig. 18).

These were the animals of an idealized life lived close to nature, woven into compositions that feel like medieval

Fig. 18 *The Farmyard*, design
for a textile or wallpaper, 1929
Hand-coloured process
engraving on paper
Victoria and Albert Museum, London
(V&A: E.332-1974)

INTRODUCTION

tapestries, or tell stories of a bucolic life in the fields and farms of the countryside. Voysey had experienced such a life in his childhood and briefly again in the years he lived at The Orchard, the house he had sold 20 years before these designs were produced.

Many of Voysey's later designs were used for wallpapers or fabrics for children's nurseries. Designers such as Walter Crane (1845–1915) had produced designs for nursery papers in the 1870s, and the work of children's illustrators such as Kate Greenaway (1846–1901) became increasingly popular in wallpapers too.[34] Voysey's designs reflect the paler colours and style of children's book illustration of the time, but the composition and line remain consistent with his earlier designs.

One of his very last designs was for a furnishing fabric based on the story of *Alice in Wonderland* (fig. 19 and plate 74), which features characterful cats, dogs and rabbits as well as lions and griffins. Voysey took inspiration for these from the famous illustrations by John Tenniel (1820–1914) for Lewis Carroll's books (published in 1865 and 1871) and then gave each of the figures and animals a new twist of personality and character.

Through his varied and characterful depiction of animals and birds in many forms Voysey created a new and radical approach to decorative design and ornament, full of delight and imagination. The effect was a fresh, bold and imaginative style that was inventive, influential and enduring. As an admiring Henry Van de Velde remarked, 'it was as if spring had come all of a sudden'.[35] And as Voysey himself wrote:

> The life of animals might be a source of stimulating joy in our own lives. We all feel a sense of pleasure when the wild birds sing, and the idea of their lovemaking and aspiring and growing more good and useful everyday is delightful, and ought to be recorded in our everyday articles of use, as well as in our natural history books.[36]

Fig. 19 Detail of *Alice in Wonderland*, c.1920 (pp. 138–9)

INTRODUCTION

Plates

All 15 birds gathered together in this design are named species that are not found together geographically. Each one is carefully observed and rich in colour, with the details and characteristics expressed in just a few lines. Voysey would draw birds such as these from specimens on display at the Natural History Museum, London, and from magazine clippings that he kept for reference. This presentation drawing was purchased from Voysey after it was displayed at the exhibition of his work at the Batsford Gallery, London, in 1931 (see fig. 2).

1. *Birds of Many Climes*, *c.*1900
Pencil, watercolour, bodycolour, pen and ink on paper
Victoria and Albert Museum, London
(V&A: Circ.768-1931)

JAPANESE ROBIN

KING BIRD OF PARADISE ARN ISLANDS.

NAG
LA NA

MEXICAN HANGNE ST COLOMBIA

HILL MYNAH N INDIA

GREEN GLOSSY STARLING

GREEN BUL BUL INDIA

ORANGE HEADED TANAGA ECUADOR

YELLOW WINGED SUG BIRD SOUTH AMER ICA

NARY

2. *The Angelic Forest*, design
for a textile or wallpaper, 1930
Print with coloured washes on paper
Royal Institute of British Architects
(RIBA: SB119/VOY[810](3))

This is one of Voysey's very late designs, and uses 12 colours,
in fashionable tones, in contrast to the more limited palette
of two or three colours that he used in the 1890s. Throughout
the design delightful birds perch and hop among the angels
of the forest, each one rendered with Voysey's characteristic
skill in observation, drawing and colour selection. His later
designs tend to be for nursery wallpapers, and the combination
of angels and birds in the forest reflects a child-friendly
interpretation of Voysey's views on the importance of faith
and nature.

3. Designs for circular badges, 1927
Hand-coloured prints on paper
Royal Institute of British Architects
(RIBA: SB117/VOY[432])

Each of these circular designs illustrates how Voysey translated his studies and sketches from life into clean, simplified but accurate depictions of birds full of character and personality. Voysey had a collection of images and studies, drawn from life, from museum specimens or magazine illustrations, which he used with endless imagination and variety in his designs for textiles, wallpapers, bookplates, badges (54, 55) and other graphic design.

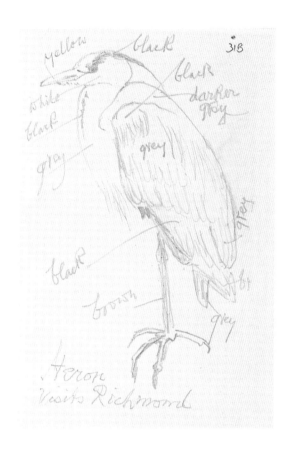

Herons feature in a number of Voysey's designs for textiles
and badges. Voysey kept a sketchbook in which he made
drawings of birds and animals. This annotated sketch is of
a heron that he observed in Richmond Park, London. Voysey
believed the heron to be attuned to his own values and belief in
individualism, describing it as a 'symbol of solitude, self-reliant
and self-sufficient. The spirit that shrinks from lime light.
The most individualistic of birds.'[37]

This technical drawing shows
the repeat and colours for
a textile or wallpaper, with
a key motif of a bird perched
on a branch. Voysey worked
quickly and in stages, building
up the composition before
converting his designs into
drawings for manufacture,
whether printing or weaving.
He had little interest in
how his designs were to be
used, and was happy to sell
his patterns even if they
were then altered to suit
different techniques.

5. *Ballad*, design for a
textile or wallpaper, 1908
Pencil and watercolour on paper
Victoria and Albert Museum, London
(V&A: E.193-1974)

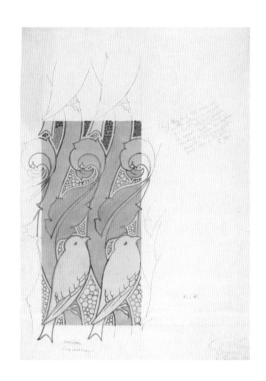

6. *Birds and Berries*, design
for a textile or wallpaper, 1897
Watercolour and pencil on paper
Victoria and Albert Museum, London
(V&A: E.151-1974)

By 1897 Voysey's design skills were at their peak, and he
was producing innovative repeating patterns with flat tonal
colourways like this with great popular success. Voysey noted,
however, that he had little or no control over the colours of
his designs when they went into production, although he did
annotate many designs in the hope of his instructions being
adhered to. For this design he gave some guidance in an
annotation for the manufacturer that reads: 'the filling in
of these seeds with another colour is a suggestion of what
to avoid. They might be composed of crossed threads of two
kinds of yellow. But they must be kept nearly the same
colour as the birds.'

7. *Birds and Berries*, furnishing
fabric, designed 1897 and manufactured
by John Duckworth & Son,
Blackburn, 1932
Woven cotton
Victoria and Albert Museum, London
(V&A: T.88-1980)

This is a trial sample by a manufacturer who had 'pirated'
a design made by Voysey 35 years earlier (6). It illustrates
just how enduring Voysey's designs were – indeed several of
his patterns for furnishing fabrics and wallpapers are still in
production today. The design is a continuation and variation
on one of Voysey's earliest designs to feature stylized birds
(25), made around 1893.

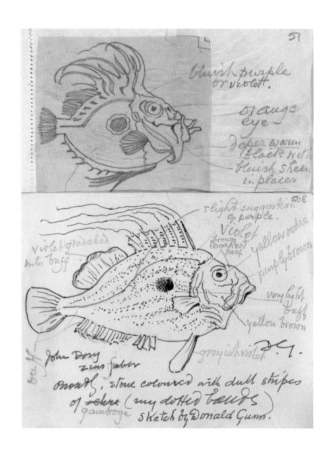

8. Drawings of fish, with annotations,
from Voysey's sketchbook, *c.*1917
Pencil and ink on paper
Royal Institute of British Architects
(RIBA: SKB458/3 p.50B/51)

These drawings of John Dory fish reveal something of Voysey's method. His starting point for including animal and bird life in his designs was to study the real thing and then abstract or simplify the form. The sketches here have been traced or given to him, and he has then made annotations about colour and pattern. A John Dory fish later became a central motif in one of his textile designs (**9**).

Designed for printed linen. C.F.A.Voysey by Voysey. F.R.I.B.A., R.D.I.

9. Design to be printed on linen, 1929
Watercolour, pencil and ink on paper
Royal Institute of British Architects
(RIBA: SB117/VOY[795](1))

This design features underwater creatures which Voysey would have compiled from different sources to create this composition, to be printed on linen. Voysey first used seahorses in a design in 1882. The watery scene is reminiscent of plates in Lydekker's *Natural History* (1896), which Voysey studied for his drawings of fish and invertebrates. The page from his sketchbook (8) shows how he ensured he was accurate in his depiction of colours and physical details.

10. Drawing of a tigress from Voysey's
sketchbook, 1917
Pencil on paper
Royal Institute of British Architects
(RIBA: SKB458/3 p.21)

Voysey made careful studies in his sketchbook of animals and
birds, making notes about colour and species. These sketches
were then translated into designs. He may have drawn this
tigress on one of his visits to London Zoo, or from a magazine
or natural history book. The tail of a tiger can be glimpsed in
a design hanging on the wall behind Voysey in the photograph
of him taken at the Batsford Gallery, London, in 1931 (fig. 2).
This may be the design by Voysey now in the collections of the
Royal Institute of British Architects featuring a tiger and a deer
and illustrating the quotation 'Sweet are the uses of adversity'
from Shakespeare's *As You Like It*.[38]

11. Design for a wallpaper, 1918
Watercolour and pencil on paper
Victoria and Albert Museum, London
(V&A: E.217-1974)

This design uses simplified motifs based on a lioness, palm trees and flowers, and a limited number of colours, to create a striking repeating pattern. The shape and stride of the lioness resemble those of the tigress he had sketched the year before (10). Voysey would often repeat motifs and adapt his ideas and sketches for use in multiple ways, which was an efficient way to work and achieved a varied output.

12. Design for a wallpaper, *c.*1905
Pen and ink and watercolour on paper
Victoria and Albert Museum, London
(V&A: Circ.42-1928)

Featuring 13 different species of birds, this repeat pattern design for a wallpaper illustrates Voysey's skilled draughtsmanship and mastery in capturing the features of birds in simple line drawings. Each bird is posed on a perch of intertwining branches and leaves, and the drawing is filled with a limited palette of colour washes, all combining to create a harmonious flat pattern. The Victoria and Albert Museum purchased this design from the exhibition of Voysey's work at the Batsford Gallery, London, in 1931 (see fig. 2).

13. Design for a textile
or wallpaper, 1926
Watercolour and pencil on paper
Victoria and Albert Museum, London
(V&A: E.280-1974)

In this design Voysey has taken the abstraction of the eagle
to an extreme, creating a strong, symmetrical repeating
pattern. The bird is still recognizable, and the background
pattern is a variation on intertwining branches; but the colour
combinations, the flattening and the repetition of form are
used to create a pattern of great effect.

14. *The Owl*, portion of a
wallpaper frieze, manufactured
by Essex & Co., 1897
Colour machine print on paper
Victoria and Albert Museum, London
(V&A: E.305-1974)

Owls featured in several of Voysey's designs for wallpaper
and textiles and he was content for the same designs to be
produced in a variety of media by different manufacturers.
This stylized owl perched in an oak tree is a motif for a
wallpaper frieze which would have been used around the
upper portion of a wall, above co-ordinating patterned
wallpaper (15). The frieze and wallpaper were published in
1899 in the *Art Journal* and also the American edition of
The Artist, which noted that the artist had conveyed the true
spirit and 'quaint humour of the owl … to give us, even in the
homeliest room, a sense of friendliness in the very walls'.[39]

15. *The Owl*, design for
a textile or wallpaper, 1897
Pencil and watercolour on paper
Victoria and Albert Museum, London
(V&A: E.263-1913)

This is one of Voysey's most recognizable and popular designs,
featuring pairs of owls with nesting chicks in shades of grey,
green and blue. Here the motif of the bird is central to the
design but is also so integrated with the pattern that it begins
to merge into abstracted shapes and colours. In Voysey's
lexicon of symbols, owls represented wisdom and often featured
in his designs. This design was produced both as a wallpaper
by Essex and Co. in 1897, and as a woollen cloth hanging by
Alexander Morton & Co. in 1898, demonstrating the variety of
applications and effects from one design idea. It was published
in several art journals at the time, including *Dekorative Kunst*,
a German magazine which dedicated a whole issue to Voysey
in 1898.[40]

hALCYONE

The halcyon (or kingfisher) was a bird that Voysey often featured in his designs. He was particularly interested in how different motifs could imbue sentiment and meaning into his work. On this design Voysey has written a long inscription referring to the Greek legend concerning Halcyon, the daughter of Aeolus, who eternally flies over the sea, seeking her drowned husband. The mythological bird of the same name, which had the power to calm the sea on which she built her nest, was described by Voysey as a 'faithful, patient bird that stills the raging of the seas, giving us halcyon days'.[41]

16. *Halcyone*, design for
a textile or wallpaper, 1898
Watercolour and pencil on paper
Victoria and Albert Museum, London
(V&A: E.152-1974)

Seagulls were another
favourite bird to feature
in Voysey's designs, and
he drew several variations
of seagull motifs between
1890 and 1905. Here they
are drawn bobbing in the
sea or perched on islands,
interwoven with pomegranate
fruits and foliage. As is usual
for Voysey, the colour palette
is limited and the motifs are
outlined in white to help
create a clear pattern. This
design went into production
as a double-cloth textile
produced by Alexander
Morton & Co., of Darvel,
Scotland. The textile was
illustrated in *Dekorative
Kunst* in 1898, in a special
issue dedicated to Voysey
and his work.[42]

17. *Sea-Gulls*, design for a textile, c.1890
Watercolour and pencil on paper
Victoria and Albert Museum, London
(V&A: E.149-1974)

'Sea Gulls'

Pl. II.

C. F. A. Voysey, Architect
11 Melina Place
St John's Wood
N.W.

18. *Sea Gulls*, design for a textile, *c.*1892
Watercolour and pencil on paper
Victoria and Albert Museum, London
(V&A: E.147-1974)

The highly stylized seagulls in this design appear to bob
happily around on the surface of the sea. The design was
produced for textile manufacturer A.H. Lee & Sons of
Birkenhead. It first came to public attention when it was
illustrated in *The Studio* in 1893 accompanying an interview
with Voysey, where he set out his views that a 'wall-paper
should be always essentially a pattern' and that 'the forms
of birds … may be used provided they are reduced to mere
symbols'. The interviewer described the colour of this paper
as a 'neutral grey-blue and in the same tone as the two
blues of the conventional sea, their yellow-green bills
being bright notes of colour'.[43]

19. Design for a wallpaper,
for Jeffrey & Co., *c*.1900
Ink wash on paper
Victoria and Albert Museum, London
(V&A: E.42-1945)

The beauty of this design lies in its strong, mirrored
horizontal repeat of pairs of birds, water lilies and foliage.
The reduction of the colours to two blue tones – dark blue
on a pale-blue ground – would have been thought very
innovative at the time and reflects Voysey's belief that
flat surfaces such as walls should also have a flat,
rather than naturalistic, pattern on them.

20. Design for a printed linen,
for G.P. & J. Baker Ltd, 1889
Watercolour and body colour on paper
Victoria and Albert Museum, London
(V&A: E.62-1961)

Voysey's design output was prolific and varied in style,
but always rooted in the same principles of simplified motifs
and a limited colour palette. The pairs of birds in this design
form the backbone of a vertical repeat, as they perch on
the twisting flower stems. The design echoes the dense
and colourful patterns based on birds, flowers and foliage
by William Morris, but flattens out the pattern to create
a more abstract, modern effect.

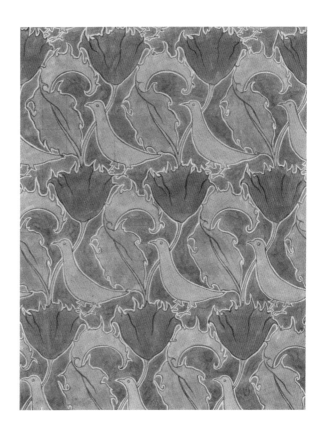

In 1913 Voysey donated a selection of about 50 designs to the Victoria and Albert Museum, including this one. Most were unsold designs that he had in his studio. Voysey worked fast and perhaps produced far more designs than he was able to sell. This one has a freshness and dynamism in its use of simplified bird and poppy motifs. Voysey favoured poppies, tulips and other home-grown flowers in his patterns, rather than the florid, hot-house species from other countries that were popular in designs of the Victorian era.

At the centre of all Voysey's pattern designs were everyday British wildlife and plants, such as blackbirds and strawberries. His lively linear drawing and fresh colour combinations established a new language in design, one that appears lighter and less naturalistic than William Morris's designs on a similar theme. This is a late design for the carpet manufacturer Tomkinson and Adam Ltd, for whom Voysey had also produced a series of original designs between 1895 and 1910, at the height of his career.

22. Design for a carpet,
for Tomkinson and Adam Ltd,
Kidderminster, Worcestershire, 1926
Watercolour and pencil on paper
Victoria and Albert Museum, London
(V&A: E.283-1974)

to Tomkinsons Ltd May 17.1928 for Carpet

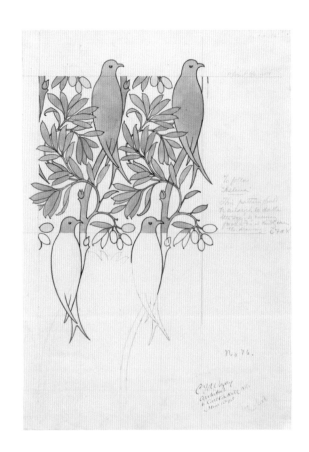

23. *Purple Bird*, design
for a furnishing fabric, 1898
Watercolour and pencil on paper
Victoria and Albert Museum, London
(V&A: E.153-1974)

Technical drawings such as this one reveal Voysey's skill
in simplifying natural bird and plant forms into graphic
elements that emphasize the repeating pattern, in contrast
to the complexity of detail in the work of his predecessors
such as William Morris. It follows Voysey's mantra that
'One leaf, one bird, one berry and one stalk can be made
an interesting pattern … but it must be conventionally
treated of course and very simple.'[44]

24. Purple Bird, furnishing
fabric, manufactured by
Alexander Morton & Co., 1899
Woven silk and wool double-cloth
Victoria and Albert Museum, London
(V&A: T.20-1953)

This textile, produced from a design of 1898 (*23*), was shown
by the manufacturer at an exhibition of the Arts and Crafts
Exhibition Society in London and retailed at Liberty & Co.
At this time Voysey was establishing himself as one of
the most original designers of his age through this kind
of repeating bird pattern, popularizing a new design
language of stylized motifs and new colours.

69

25. *Birds and Berries*, design
for a wallpaper, *c*.1893
Watercolour and pencil on paper
Victoria and Albert Museum, London
(V&A: E.145-1974)

From the outset of his career Voysey established a formula
for a repeating pattern based on a pair of birds perched on a
twisting stem or branch, with berries and flowers. This design
was reproduced to accompany an interview with Voysey in
The Studio in 1893. His work was regularly featured in the
magazine from then on, which did much to spread knowledge
of his designs and advance his reputation, especially in Europe.
The interviewer noted that Voysey's designs 'owe so much
to their colour' and described how the harmony of 'the deep
yellow of the birds, perched on pale green stalks among berries
of salmon and creamy yellow, is balanced by the blue-green
of the conventional leaf form'.[45]

26. Design for a textile
or wallpaper, *c.*1893–6
Watercolour on paper
Victoria and Albert Museum, London
(V&A: E.146-1974)

In this design Voysey has created a repeating pattern from
a bird in a tree by the water's edge, with a forest and distant
shore above. Although this is a landscape scene, the perspective
has been flattened to emphasize the repeating motifs. Voysey
did not believe in the principle of applying patterns with
perspective and depth to flat surfaces such as walls. The
design was published in *The Studio* magazine in 1896.

Voysey designed across many different media, but the
language of his design remained consistent in everything he
did. He used his designs to convey symbolic meaning. Here the
angel and dove are used to represent gentleness, the overall
theme of the stained-glass panel. The drawing style, with
thick heavy lines demarcating the window lead, pale washes
of colour, and some detail and pattern created with fine
black line drawing, reflects both the technical requirements
of making a stained-glass window and the simplicity of
expression found in Voysey's designs for other media.

28. *St Cecilia*, design for
a bookplate, *c.*1890–1900
Watercolour and ink on paper
Crab Tree Farm

St Cecilia is the patron saint of music, and this design was used
by Voysey as the central image in a design for a bookplate for
Trinity College of Music, London. The 'halo' effect of a tightly
packed flock of flying birds was a device that is particularly
associated with Voysey. He wrote a poem on the reverse:

> Listen to the music of my heart
> Which birds do bring upon the wing
> All I would sing
> If only I with subtle art
> Could reach your heart.

29. Design for 'The New
Silk Cloth', 1901
Pencil and watercolour on paper
Victoria and Albert Museum, London
(V&A: E.188-1974)

Birds in flight, combined with hearts, were one of Voysey's
most distinctive and innovative design motifs, which he
first introduced in the 1880s and worked in many variations
afterwards. The lightness of touch and sense of movement had
their origins in the work of A.H. Mackmurdo, who taught him
how to design for pattern, but Voysey advanced the concept
with his complete flattening of the perspective and colour.

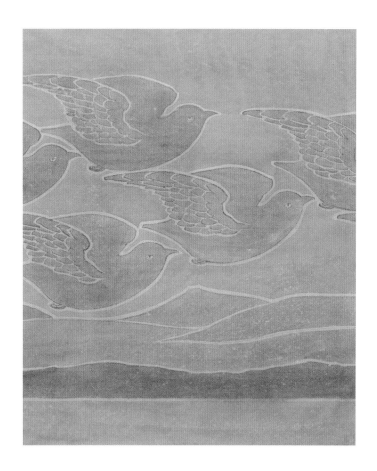

30. *Helena*, design for a textile
or wallpaper, 1901
Pencil and watercolour on paper
Victoria and Albert Museum, London
(V&A: E.189-1974)

This scene of gold birds flying above fields and hills was drawn
when Voysey was at the peak of his success. It is a confident
and highly simplified pattern, with a white outline used to
emphasize the shapes and colours. Voysey's birds evolved from
flighty, naturalistic depictions to these bold, abstracted forms
flocking together in dynamic groups.

31. *The Savaric*, portion of wallpaper, produced by Essex & Co., *c.*1897
Colour woodblock print on paper
Victoria and Albert Museum, London
(V&A: E.1895-1953)

The block repeat of birds in flight and trees creates a dramatic effect of movement in this wallpaper. The use of just two shades of blue lends itself very well to the non-mechanical technique of woodblock printing. This design was published internationally, including in the German publication *Dekorative Kunst* in 1898, which dedicated a whole issue to Voysey. *The House* magazine noted in 1903 that 'none has displayed more marked individuality than Mr. C.F.A. Voysey … that his work may be recognised at a glance', describing *The Savaric* as 'one of many evidences of this artist's delight in introducing bird forms to his studies'.[46]

32. *The Fairyland*, portion of wallpaper,
manufactured by Essex & Co., 1896
Colour machine print on paper
Victoria and Albert Museum, London
(V&A: Circ.262-1953)

This design features an arc of doves in flight through a forest
planted with mushrooms and hyacinth. The natural elements
of the design are identifiable even though the motifs are
stylized, and the effect is intended to emphasize the overall
pattern. The wallpaper was produced by a machine-roller,
which is more suited than woodblock printing (31) to the
complexity and density of the pattern, although Voysey has
characteristically used a limited number of colours in muted
tones. The same design, in a different colourway, was also
produced as a woven furnishing fabric.[47]

This design has a repeating motif of a bird in flight, carrying a flower across a hilly landscape. The title name, Ailsa, is a traditional Scottish girl's name, and may also refer to Ailsa Craig, a rocky island in the Firth of Clyde, close to Darvel in east Ayrshire, where this fabric was produced. The same design was used for a wallpaper frieze made by Essex & Co., titled 'Sparrow', which was published in the *Journal of Decorative Art* in 1896. The commentator noted that 'one feels the joyful spirit of those little birds animating us as we gaze upon it'.[48]

33. *Ailsa*, furnishing fabric, manufactured by Alexander Morton & Co., *c.*1900
Tapestry woven wool and cotton double cloth
Victoria and Albert Museum, London
(V&A: Circ.97-1966)

34. *Tree and Swallows*, design
for a woollen furnishing fabric,
for Alexander Morton & Co., 1899
Watercolour and pencil on paper
Victoria and Albert Museum, London
(V&A: E.156-1974)

The device of a tree with birds circling or flocking around it
was one of Voysey's trademark innovations. He designed many
variations on the theme, some tightly drawn and simplified like
this one, and others more lightly drafted and more obviously
sketched from nature. This design was sold to Alexander
Morton & Co. to weave into a woollen double-cloth furnishing
fabric with a bold repeating pattern. The Victoria and Albert
Museum has a sample of the cloth in its collections[49] which
was published in *Deutsche Kunst und Dekoration* in 1903.[50]

35. *The Birds Upon the Trees*,
design for a cretonne, 1918
Pencil and watercolour on paper
Victoria and Albert Museum, London
(V&A: E.203-1974)

Each of the birds in this design is different, showing the
variety and interest Voysey was able to create with simple
shapes, a few lines and one flat colour. Voysey also produced
several variations on the theme of birds perched in branches,
for wallpapers and fabrics. This pattern was designed for a
cretonne, a strong cotton or linen cloth used for curtains
and upholstery.

While Voysey's designs often appear very simple, they are carefully constructed in consideration of the pattern and repeat. His view that 'Elaboration is easy … simplicity requires perfection' was quoted when this design was published to accompany an article about his wallpaper designs in an American furnishing magazine in 1905.[51] The lightness of line and simple colours of the birds, flowers and leaves give a fresh, light feeling and encapsulate the inspiration of nature and in particular of English natural life.

36. *Early English Design*, for a furnishing fabric or wallpaper, 1899
Watercolour and pencil on paper
Victoria and Albert Museum, London
(V&A: E.175-1974)

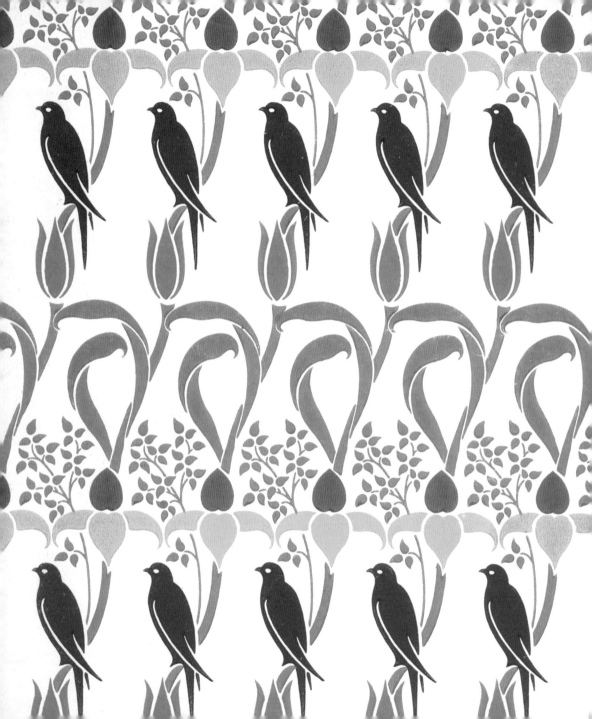

The strong horizontal lines of repeating pattern, simplified motifs and flat bright colours seen in this wallpaper could not have been more of a radical departure from the florid and blowsy wallpaper designs that were fashionable in the previous decades. This was a new design language for the new century, but still rooted in Voysey's Gothic-inspired principles of simplicity and fitness for purpose. The bright colours and delicate detail suited the machine-roller printing technique. The design was published in the *Decorators and Painters Magazine* in 1902–3.

37. *The Minto*, portion of wallpaper, produced by Essex & Co., 1901
Colour machine print on paper
Victoria and Albert Museum, London
(V&A: E.311-1974)

The repeat here has distinct horizontal and vertical lines, made from a single motif of bird, leaf and berries. The simplicity of design and use of just three harmonious colours were well suited to modern printing techniques. Voysey understood how to design for manufacturing and although he rarely had any input or influence on the final colours or production, he wanted to influence the taste of both manufacturer and customer. The design was one of several published in 1905 in the American magazine *The Upholstery Dealer and Decorative Furnisher*, to accompany an article which profiled him as 'the outstanding personality' among 'modern British designers'.[52]

38. Portion of wallpaper, produced by Essex & Co., 1901
Colour machine print on paper
Victoria and Albert Museum, London
(V&A: E.315-1974)

39. Design for a wallpaper
or textile, 1901
Pencil and watercolour on paper
Victoria and Albert Museum, London
(V&A: E.184–1974)

Blackbirds and rooks were among the birds Voysey
particularly liked to depict. Here the repetition of the
same bird motif creates a lively rhythm against the highly
abstracted landscape of a ploughed field and trees. A familiar
agricultural or countryside scene has been transformed
by flattening it to make it appropriate for decorative use
and to maximize the repeating effect of the pattern.

40. *Cornfield*, design
for a wallpaper, 1920
Pencil and watercolour on paper
Victoria and Albert Museum, London
(V&A: E.266-1974)

Here we can see Voysey's use of symbolism and knowledge
of heraldry applied to stylized motifs from nature to create
a modern decorative effect. The sheaves of corn are symbols
of plenty and the rook is also associated with myths and
symbolism, good and bad. The lighter yellow background
is typical of his designs of this later date. The design was
published in *Good Furniture Magazine* in November 1924,
making the connection that 'In pattern designing a symbolism
akin to that of heraldry may recall scenes in nature that have
given pleasure.'[53]

41. Design for a textile, 1920
Pencil and watercolour on paper
Victoria and Albert Museum, London
(V&A: E.263-1974)

This design for a repeat pattern features a motif of an eagle perched on a rock against a watery background. The eagle is drawn with precision in thick, emphatic black lines. In Voysey's language of symbolism eagles represented wisdom and were birds he thought to be noble, dignified and godlike.

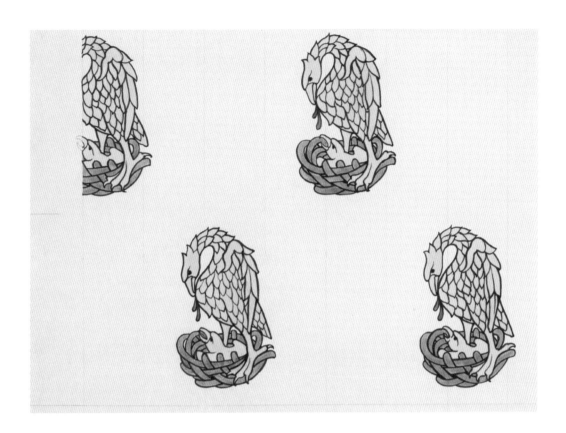

42. Design for a textile showing
the pelican in her piety, 1919
Pencil and watercolour on paper
Victoria and Albert Museum, London
(V&A: E.262-1974)

The device of a pelican plucking her breast to feed her young
with her own blood has been in use as a symbol of charity,
self-sacrifice or Christian ritual since medieval times. It is
commonly used in heraldry, a subject that Voysey studied
and translated into some of his design work. This design
for a textile features a single repeating motif of the pelican
and her nest. A similar motif appears in a number of Voysey's
other designs, including several wallpaper designs (43) and
the bookplate he designed for his son Annesley.[54]

43. *Fidelis*, design for a wallpaper, 1919
Hand-coloured process engraving
on paper
Victoria and Albert Museum, London
(V&A: E.322-1974)

This wallpaper design includes a pelican – a symbol of self-sacrifice – and the Latin word *fidelis*, which means 'always faithful'. It was probably made to commemorate the sacrifice made by the men and women who died in the First World War. In 1919 Voysey contributed designs to the exhibitions at the Victoria and Albert Museum and Royal Academy, London, which were organized by the War Memorials Committee to facilitate the commissioning of memorials to approved designs.

44. *The Heron*, textile design, 1919
Pencil and watercolour on paper
Victoria and Albert Museum, London
(V&A E.295-1974)

This late design is lighter and more linear than Voysey's designs of the 1890s, showing how his style evolved and changed, especially in his later years. The pattern is delicately drawn and relies, like his earlier designs, on the composition of a bird and tree, with suggestions of water and grass in just three simple colours. Voysey made sketches of herons from life (4) and believed them to be the most individualistic of birds.

45. *The Squire's Garden*,
portion of wallpaper,
produced by Essex & Co., 1896
Colour machine print,
on paper, varnished
Victoria and Albert Museum, London
(V&A: E.1924-1934)

Peacocks were one of Voysey's favourite birds, symbolizing protection, integrity and longevity. This composition marks a new, lighter approach to bringing different elements together to create a more pictorial effect rather than a rigid repeating pattern. It is reminiscent of an embroidered sampler, and a similar design[55] was also embroidered for use as a bed quilt by the eminent embroiderer Annie Reynolds-Stevens (1896–1925). Voysey used this wallpaper to decorate his children's Play and Schoolroom at The Orchard, Chorleywood (fig. 16). He was interested in the economics of house building and decoration, and wallpaper was an affordable option for someone on a limited budget, as he was.

Mirrored pairs of peacocks among flowers and foliage form
the central motif of this repeating pattern. A white line around
the pattern creates clarity and space in what otherwise would
be a rather dense and similarly toned pattern. The names of
Voysey's patterns often have meaning or make reference to a
place. Tierney is Irish for lord, and Voysey had also lived and
worked at Tierney Road, Streatham, between 1888 and 1891.

46. *The Tierney*, portion of wallpaper,
produced by Essex & Co., *c.*1897
Colour woodblock print on paper
Victoria and Albert Museum, London
(V&A: E.1894-1953)

47. Textile design, 1919
Pencil and watercolour on paper
Victoria and Albert Museum, London
(V&A: E.244-1974)

This design relies on the very simple effect of three colours and plenty of white space. The bird in the grass among tulips is full of life and character, but is almost stencil-like in its execution. Voysey believed that a pattern such as this is more pleasing when it contains no more than the 'simple expression of one or two ideas'.[56]

48. *The Merle*, portion of wallpaper,
produced by Essex & Co., 1901
Colour woodblock print on paper
Victoria and Albert Museum, London
(V&A: E.1884–1953)

This design relies on a limited number of colours, and the
motifs of birds and irises are reduced to flat shapes and washes
of colour on a pale ground. The birds are merles, from the
blackbird family. The simplicity of the design, with just four
colours including the background and bold shapes with limited
detail, was perfectly suited to woodblock printing by hand.
Essex & Co. specialized in this technique and preferred it to
machine-roller printing.

C.F.A.Voysey Architect.
98 York Place.
September.
1907.

49. *Fool's Parsley*, wallpaper
design for Sanderson & Sons, 1907
Pencil, watercolour and Indian
ink on paper
Victoria and Albert Museum, London
(V&A: E.265-1913)

The design is symmetrically arranged across a vertical axis,
with canaries perched on a toxic plant called fool's parsley
which grows on verges and wastelands. This was one of
Voysey's most mature designs, produced for Arthur Sanderson
& Sons, for whom he had been designing wallpapers since 1887.
Voysey's long-standing relationship with Sandersons led him to
design a new block as an extension to their factory in Chiswick,
London, in 1902, one of only a small number of commercial
buildings undertaken by him.

This collection of garden birds, butterflies, insects and flowers celebrates the natural world and the flora and fauna of an English country garden. Voysey was adept at observing the natural world and the things he could see around him, translating plants and creatures into simple and colourful motifs and arranging them on a page to create a pattern full of life and vibrancy.

50. Design for a textile, 1919
Pencil and watercolour on paper
Victoria and Albert Museum, London
(V&A: E.247-1974)

This quintessential furnishing fabric, in fresh, bright colours, depicts an idealized country meadow or garden with a repeating pattern of birds and flowers. It is a good example of how Voysey always designed with the principal emphasis on the effect of the pattern.

51. *Pastoral*, furnishing fabric, manufactured by Morton Sundour Fabrics Ltd, Edinburgh, 1920s
Roller-printed cotton
Victoria and Albert Museum, London
(V&A: Circ.857-1967)

52. Design for a textile pattern for
G.P. & J. Baker Ltd, London, 1889
Watercolour and body colour
on tracing paper
Victoria and Albert Museum, London
(V&A: E.60-1961)

This early experimental design was drawn during Voysey's
first ten years as an architect and pattern designer.
The fluid whiplash lines of the snake entwined in tulips
show the influence of his friend and teacher A.H. Mackmurdo.
Decorative designs based on snakes, invertebrates and
underwater creatures became popular, especially among
European designers such as Herman Obrist (1862–1927),
as new books on natural history and sea creatures were
published in the 1860s and 1870s.

53. Design for a velvet tablecloth,
produced by G.P. & J. Baker Ltd,
London, 1888
Body colour on paper
Victoria and Albert Museum, London
(V&A: E.59-1961)

Produced as a printed velvet tablecloth in a single colour,
this design features seahorses and octopuses among seaweed,
unusually combined with a border of fantastic birds similar to
those Voysey used in a later design (20). Voysey later turned
to books such as *The Royal Natural History* (1896) to study
and draw sea creatures and other invertebrates.

54. Designs for circular badges showing animals, sea creatures and birds, 1927
Watercolour, pencil and ink on paper
Royal Institute of British Architects
(RIBA: VOY[432])

55. Designs for circular badges showing animals and flowers, 1927
Watercolour, pencil and ink on paper
Royal Institute of British Architects
(RIBA: VOY[432])

Each of these beautiful depictions captures the anatomy and characteristics of the animal or bird, imbuing them with a distinct personality. The creatures, including a squirrel, rat, monkey, polar bear, rabbits and hares, a dog and a beetle, appear throughout Voysey's pattern designs, and were also used symbolically in his designs for bookplates or badges (see plate 3).

C. J. A. Voysey 1927

C. J. A. Voysey 1927

(. J. A. Voysey. 192)

C. J. A. Voysey.

(. J. A. Voysey. 192)

C. J. A. Voysey 1927.

56. Design for a wallpaper, *c*.1884–9
Watercolour and pencil on paper
Royal Institute of British Architects, London
(RIBA: SB119/VOY[863B])

This is one of Voysey's very earliest designs, featuring a writhing dragon and shooting flames. Stylistically it has more affinity with the designs of Voysey's friend and teacher of pattern design A.H. Mackmurdo. The colours are rich and jewel-like, including metallic gold, and ink marks convey the detail of the dragon's scales. The design is perhaps experimental, and shows us Voysey stretching his legs and familiarizing himself with the new genre of pattern-making. His later designs are much more muted and simplified.

57. Design for a wool-work panel, 1918
Gouache on paper
Victoria and Albert Museum, London
(V&A: E.5184-1919)

Voysey produced many designs for memorials, ranging
from funerary urns and gravestones to war memorials and
wallpaper designs (43). This included a number of designs
commemorating the First World War. This unusually bold
and brightly coloured design for wool-work depicts the
winged angel St Michael slaying a dragon, a Christian image
symbolizing the vanquishing of Satan. Voysey contributed it
to the Victoria and Albert Museum exhibition in 1919
promoting suitable designs for war memorials.

58. Design for a wallpaper
or textile, 1920
Watercolour and pencil on paper
Victoria and Albert Museum, London
(V&A: E.269-1974)

Voysey's use of woodland animals such as squirrels as design
motifs was in line with Arts and Crafts ideas, but was also
thought to be innovative and radical in the commercial world
of manufacture. His treatment of the motifs here was to refine
the squirrel, acorns and branches to strong curved lines.
The limited colour palette makes the repeating pattern
more abstract.

59. Design for a wallpaper, 1929
Watercolour, pencil, pen and
ink on paper
Victoria and Albert Museum, London
(V&A: Circ.44-1928)

Combinations of birds with animals such as squirrels were
the mainstay of Voysey's pattern designs. Here the colours
are fashionably toned down, and the birds and squirrels are
simplified to motifs yet still true to their species. The design
is inscribed: 'This drawing is to be returned to the author as
agreed Nov 23 1929 / sold to Speed for wallpaper Nov 1923.'

Repeat 17 inches straight across x 12". 11 prints producing 12 different colours.

The flattened perspective of this simplified farmyard scene was quite radical for pattern design of the time. The design is packed with individual scenes and motifs that conjure up an idyllic image of life on the farm, a long way from the reality of Voysey's urban London life. Details such as the maid milking a cow occur in other Voysey designs, and the cockerel weather vane was made in wrought iron for one of the houses he designed.

60. Design depicting a farmyard, 1925
Watercolour and pencil on paper
Victoria and Albert Museum, London
(V&A: E.326-1974)

61. *Let Us Prey*, design
for a wallpaper, 1909
Watercolour on paper
Victoria and Albert Museum, London
(V&A: E.638-1937)

This design is full of Voysey's characteristic humour and wit.
The quirky pattern of a cat, bird and worm, surrounded by
flowers and leaves, illustrates the ascending food chain. Even
when Voysey uses motifs of ordinary domestic animals and
birds, the structure of the pattern retains a strong repeat and
distinct vertical alignment, combined with bright, flat colours.

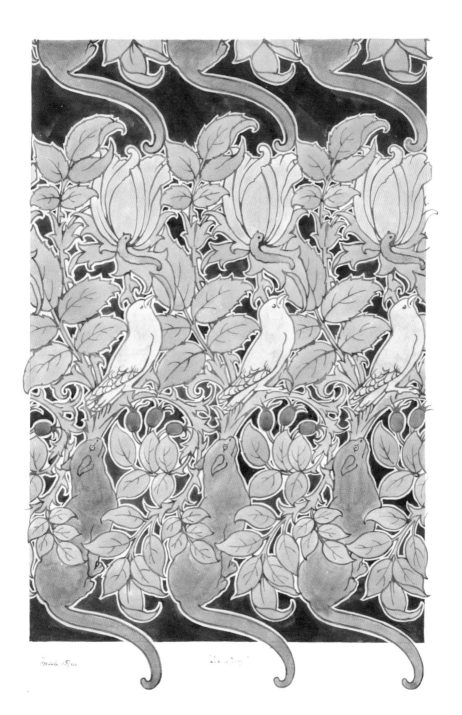

62. *I Love Little Pussy*, design
for a wallpaper or textile, 1895
Watercolour and pencil on paper
Royal Institute of British Architects, London
(RIBA: SB119/VOY[839])

Voysey's animals are often shown in humorous compositions, inspired by rhymes or mottos. This design for a nursery wallpaper features a cat being tempted by the opportunity to catch birds and mice. It is one of several designs by Voysey which feature animals, especially cats, and are based on popular poems, in this case 'I Love Little Pussy':

> I love little pussy,
> Her coat is so warm,
> And if I don't hurt her,
> She'll do me no harm.
> So I'll not pull her tail,
> Nor drive her away,
> But pussy and I,
> Very gently will play.

63. *Huntsman*, design
for a wallpaper, 1919
Hand-coloured process
engraving on paper
Victoria and Albert Museum, London
(V&A: E.321-1974)

Here Voysey has depicted a hunting scene in a repeating
pattern which features an archer and his dogs hunting a stag,
surrounded by birds in the trees, and along the banks of a fish-
filled river which flows past a castle. The design is reminiscent
of medieval tapestry but is rendered in unusual colours and
with a light touch that makes it appear modern, fresh
and full of life.

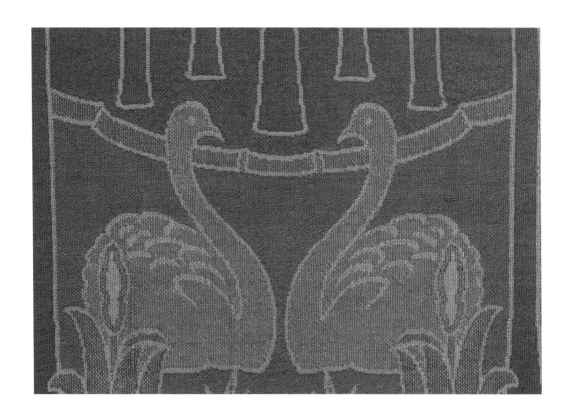

64. *Duleek* hanging, manufactured
by Alexander Morton & Co. and sold
by Liberty & Co. Ltd, 1896–1900
Jacquard-woven woollen double cloth
Victoria and Albert Museum, London
(V&A: Circ.886-1967)

The central motifs of this design are stags and swans in
a forest, with birds in flight above the treetops. It was perhaps
one of Voysey's most popular and adaptable designs, which
was widely published. It was first used for wallpaper and
later adapted for wallpaper friezes and woven textiles
and carpets. 'Duleek' is the name of a village in County
Meath, Ireland, and is taken from the Irish word meaning
'house of stones', referring to an early church built in the
village. We do not know much about how Voysey's designs
were named, but they often have Irish or Scottish associations.

65. *Ballad*, design for a tapestry, 1902
Pencil and watercolour on paper
Victoria and Albert Museum, London
(V&A: E.191-1974)

The poses and characteristics of the deer in this design are
rendered with a lightness of touch and keen observational
skills. Voysey may have watched the deer in Richmond Park
in south-west London, which he visited from time to time. The
style of the composition is reminiscent of early embroideries
on linen. A roller-printed linen of this design was produced
by Morton Sundour Fabrics Ltd in 1930.

The movement of deer
leaping through a bluebell
wood is captured in this
delicately abstracted design.
It was intended for a
cretonne, a type of linen or
cotton often used for curtains
or upholstery. Drawn in
1918, the design illustrates
Voysey's career-long interest
in subjects based on nature
and the countryside. It is
confidently but delicately
drawn, with repeating motifs
such as the deer previously
used in other designs (**65, 71**)
set in a dense but carefully
drawn pattern of intertwining
trees and occasional precisely
placed bluebells.

66. *The Deer in the Forest,*
design for a cretonne, 1918
Watercolour and pencil on paper
Victoria and Albert Museum, London
(V&A: E.205-1974)

67. Design for an Australian
postage stamp, 1911
Pen and ink over pencil on paper
Victoria and Albert Museum, London
(V&A: E.298-1913)

In 1911 the Australian Postmaster-General's Department
held a design competition for a series of new Commonwealth
postage stamps. This is Voysey's entry, and he naturally turned
to 'the peculiar and familiar emblems' of a kangaroo and
eucalyptus surrounded by 'wheat sheaves to suggest the great
agricultural interest of that great Island'.[57] Voysey would have
been able to see a kangaroo in London Zoo, which had five
different varieties of the species at that time.

68. Advertisement for Essex & Co.
Wallpaper Manufacturers, *c*.1899
Line-block on paper
British Museum
(BM: 1937,1106.17)

Voysey was skilled in lettering and graphic design. In this
advertisement for the wallpaper manufacturer Essex & Co.,
he has created an image of rustic charm with a figure of
a shepherd leading his flock of sheep through a meadow.
The Westminster Wallpapers advertised here were a collection
of over 150 designs for wallpapers by some of the leading
names of the Arts and Crafts Movement. In 1900 Voysey
was contracted by Essex & Co. to produce 30 designs a year.

69. Design with piper in a tree
with birds and animals, 1919
Pencil and watercolour on paper
Victoria and Albert Museum, London
(V&A: E.256-1974)

The composition of a piper in a tree with an assembly of
animal and bird motifs was one that Voysey developed at the
start of his design life, and continued to use with variations
throughout his career. The repeating animal motifs are
conveyed to great effect in simple line drawings.

70. *Green Pastures*, carpet sample,
manufactured by Tomkinson
& Adam Ltd, 1896
Knotted wool
Victoria and Albert Museum, London
(V&A: T.72-1953)

This design shows Voysey at his most innovative and radical.
He has created a flat repeating pattern of trees and sheep,
which at the time would have seemed most incongruous for
a carpet. In 1896, *The Studio* magazine described this design
as 'distinctly ingenious', yet commented that 'possibly after
more familiarity we could accept it as legitimate; but at
present it seems unorthodox … and although it pleases you
aesthetically, it would be too great a shock to one's theory
to praise it unreservedly'.[58]

71. Design for *River Rug*, 1903
Watercolour on paper
Crab Tree Farm

This unique design is full of rich detail, including many of Voysey's characteristic motifs of birds and animals, such as black and white swans, geese, a peacock, blackbirds, cows, pigs, sheep and deer being hunted by figures on horseback, along the banks of a meandering river seen from above. It was probably designed and made as a hearth rug for Voysey's family home, The Orchard (fig. 16). The aerial perspective was perhaps inspired by a series of tapestry maps in the collections of the Victoria and Albert Museum, made in the Sheldon factory, Worcestershire, in the late sixteenth century.

72. *In My Orchard*, design
for a textile or wallpaper, 1929
Hand-coloured process
engraving on paper
Victoria and Albert Museum, London
(V&A: E.333-1974)

Voysey's drawing style remained consistent throughout
his career. The colours in this late design have been subtly
adjusted to the lighter palette in vogue in the late 1920s.
The title suggests nostalgia for the semi-rural life that
Voysey briefly experienced at his home The Orchard
(fig. 16), which he could not afford to maintain, and
sold over 20 years earlier.

The composition and line of this late design remain consistent with earlier designs. Voysey produced multiple variations on the same motifs. Later designs such as this one were produced for use as wallpaper or fabrics in children's nurseries, and are reminiscent of children's book illustration of the same period.

73. *Woodland Notes*, design
for a textile or wallpaper, 1929
Hand-coloured process engraving
Victoria and Albert Museum, London
(V&A: E.329-1974)

This was one of Voysey's most popular late designs for a children's nursery fabric. The pattern is based on the tale of *Alice in Wonderland*, and features cats, dogs and rabbits as well as a walrus, lions and griffins. Voysey traced the figures from John Tenniel's classic illustrations for Lewis Carroll's book, published in 1865, and then gave them a new twist of personality and character.

74. *Alice in Wonderland*, furnishing fabric, manufactured by Morton Sundour Fabrics Ltd, *c.*1920
Roller-printed cotton chintz
Victoria and Albert Museum, London
(V&A: Circ.856-1967)

Notes

1 Robert Donat, 'Uncle Charles', *The Architects' Journal*, vol. XCII (20 March 1941), p. 194

2 Voysey 1930–32

3 See for example RIBA Drawings Collection, VOY[581], Design for an invitation or ticket to Bedford Park Fancy Dress Ball, 19 June 1895

4 RIBA Drawings Collection, VOY[709]9

5 Voysey 1895, p. 82

6 E.B.S. 1896, p. 209

7 Quoted in Richardson 1965, p. 403

8 Voysey 1909, p. 135

9 Fletcher 1931, p. 764

10 See examples in the V&A collections including E.3654-2007

11 Bock 1966, p. vi

12 Quoted in Whitworth Art Gallery 1969, p. 10

13 Quoted in Bock 1966, p. 31

14 Brandon-Jones n.d. [1957], p. 244

15 Anon. 1893

16 Ibid., p. 236

17 Livingstone with Donnelly and Parry 2016, p. 60

18 Ibid., p. 164

19 Voysey 1909, p. 136

20 *The Studio*, 28, no. 119 (February 1903), p. 35

21 Livingstone and Parry 2005, p. 129

22 Voysey 1909, p. 136

23 C.F.A. Voysey, 'The value of hidden influences as disclosed in the life of one ordinary man', unpublished typescript, RIBA VOC/4/6 (1931), pp. 1–2

24 Ibid., p. 1

25 Voysey 1901

26 For example Expense to Zoological Gardens to Study Eagles (17 February 1908), Professional Expenses 1 January 1906–1940, RIBA VOC/2/1

27 Voysey 1930–32

28 'Report of speech given at "Dinner to C.F. Annesley Voysey"', *Journal of the Royal Institute of British Architects*, vol. 35 (1927), p. 53

29 Anon. 1893

30 Anon., 'C.F.A. Voysey: the man and his work', *The Architect and Building News*, vol. 117, part 5 (4 March 1927), p. 405

31 Voysey 1930–32

32 'The Arts and Crafts Exhibition', *The Artist*, XVIII (July–December 1896), pp. 20–22

33 C.F.A. Voysey, 'L'Art Nouveau: what it is and what is thought of it: a symposium', *Magazine of Art*, vol. 2 (1904), p. 211

34 Oman and Hamilton 1982, p. 67

35 Nikolaus Pevsner, *The Sources of Modern Architecture and Design* (Thames & Hudson, London, 1968), p. 68

36 Voysey 1909, p. 136

37 RIBA Drawings Collection, VOY[506]

38 RIBA Drawings Collection, VOY[637]17

39 'Some new English wall papers', *The Artist: An Illustrated Monthly Record of Arts, Crafts and Industries* (American edition), vol. 25, no. 233 (May–June 1899), p. 48

40 'Voysey Heft' 1898, p. 273

41 Voysey 1930–32, no. 36

42 'Voysey Heft' 1898, p. 265

43 Anon. 1893, p. 235

44 'The work of Mr C. F. A. Voysey', *The House*, vol. 4, no. XXIII (January 1899), p. 163

45 Anon. 1893

46 'On the choice of wallpapers', *The House* (1903), p. 111

47 See example in V&A collections: Circ.95-1966

48 'Paper-hangings in 1896: Essex & Co. in 1896', *Journal of Decorative Art* (January 1896), p. 19

49 V&A: T.13-1953

50 'Morris, Walter Crane, Ashbee, Voysey, und die Englische Abteilung in Turin 1902', *Deutsche Kunst und Dekoration*, vol. 11, no. 5 (February 1903), p. 233

Picture Credits

51 J. Taylor, 'C. F. A. Voysey', *The Upholstery Dealer and Decorative Furnisher* [New York], vol. 7 (1905), p. 26

52 Ibid., pp. 19–26

53 C.A. Hindley, 'The use of colour in decorative furnishing, a series of practical lessons: lesson V', *Good Furniture Magazine* (November 1924), p. 236

54 Voysey 1930–32, no. 29

55 RIBA Drawings Collection, VOY[670]

56 Anon. 1893, p. 233

57 Voysey 1930–32, no. 16

58 Anon., 'The Arts and Crafts Exhibition 1896 (third notice)', *The Studio*, vol. 9 (1896), pp. 194–5

Selected Bibliography

Anon., 'An interview with Mr. Charles F. Annesley Voysey, architect and designer', *The Studio*, vol. 1, no. 1 (April 1893), pp. 235–6

Judith Bock, 'The wallpaper designs of C.F.A. Voysey' (MA thesis, New York University, 1966)

John Brandon-Jones, *C.F.A. Voysey: A Memoir* (Architectural Association, London, n.d. [1957])

John Brandon-Jones et al., *C.F.A. Voysey: Architect and Designer, 1857–1941* (Lund Humphries in association with Art Gallery and Museums and the Royal Pavilion, Brighton; London, 1978)

Stuart Durant, *The Decorative Designs of C.F.A. Voysey: From the Drawings Collection of the British Architectural Library, the Royal Institute of British Architects* (RIBA, London, 1990)

H.M. Fletcher, 'The work of C.F.A. Voysey', *Journal of the Royal Institute of British Architects*, vol. 38 (1931), pp. 763–4

Peter Floud, *Catalogue of an Exhibition of Victorian and Edwardian Decorative Arts* (Victoria and Albert Museum, London, 1952)

Peter Floud, 'The wallpaper designs of C.F.A. Voysey', *The Penrose Annual*, vol. 52 (1958), pp. 10–14

D. Gebhard, *Charles F.A. Voysey* (Hennessey & Ingalls, Los Angeles, 1975)

Wendy Hitchmough, *C.F.A. Voysey* (Phaidon, London, 1995)

Hunterian Art Gallery (University of Glasgow), *C.F.A. Voysey : Decorative Design* (exhib. cat., Glasgow, 1993)

Karen Livingstone, *The Bookplates and Badges of C.F.A. Voysey, Architect and Designer of the Arts and Crafts Movement* (Antique Collectors' Club, Woodbridge, 2011)

Karen Livingstone, *V&A Pattern: C.F.A. Voysey* (V&A Publications, London, 2013)

Karen Livingstone and Linda Parry (eds), *International Arts and Crafts* (V&A Publications, London, 2005)

Karen Livingstone, with Max Donnelly and Linda Parry, *C.F.A. Voysey: Arts & Crafts Designer* (V&A Publications, London, 2016)

Charles C. Oman and Jean Hamilton, *Wallpapers: A History and Illustrated Catalogue of the Collection of the Victoria and Albert Museum* (Sotheby's Publications in association with the Victoria and Albert Museum, London, 1982)

Linda Parry, *Textiles of the Arts & Crafts Movement* (Thames & Hudson, London, 1996)

Margaret Richardson, 'Wallpapers by C.F.A. Voysey', *Journal of the Royal Institute of British Architects*, vol. 72 (1965), pp. 399–403

E.B.S., 'Some recent designs by Mr C.F.A. Voysey', *The Studio*, vol. 7 (1896), pp. 209–18

Duncan Simpson, *C.F.A. Voysey: An Architect of Individuality* (Lund Humphries, London, 1979)

Joanna Symonds, *Catalogue of the Drawings Collection of the Royal Institute of British Architects: C.F.A. Voysey* (RIBA, Farnborough, 1976)

C.F.A. Voysey, 'The aims and conditions of the modern decorator', *Journal of Decorative Art*, vol. 15 (1895), pp. 82–90

C.F.A. Voysey, 'The Orchard, Chorleywood, Herts', *Architectural Review*, vol. 10 (1901), pp. 32–8

C.F.A. Voysey, 'Ideas in things', in *The Arts Connected with Building: Lectures on Craftsmanship and Design delivered at Carpenters' Hall, London Wall for the Worshipful Co of Carpenters*, ed. T. Raffles Davison (B.T. Batsford, London, 1909), pp. 101–38

C.F.A. Voysey, *Individuality* (Elkin Matthews, London, 1915)

C.F.A. Voysey, '1874 & after', *Architectural Review*, vol. 70 (1931), pp. 91–2

C.F.A. Voysey, 'Symbolism in Design', unpublished manuscript, RIBA SKB458/2 (1930–32)

C.F.A. Voysey, *Catalogue of an Exhibition of the Works of C.F. Annesley Voysey FRIBA at the Batsford Gallery, 15 North Audley Street, London W1, October 2 to 17, 1931*, with a foreword by Edwin Lutyens

Acknowledgments

Author's Biography

'Voysey Heft', *Dekorative Kunst: Illustrierte Zeitschrift für angewandte Kunst*, vol. 1, no. 6 (March 1898) [issue devoted to Voysey]

Clive Wainwright, *Architect-Designers, Pugin to Mackintosh: 5–29 May 1981, the Fine Art Society Ltd with Haslam & Whiteway Ltd* (exhib. cat., Fine Art Society, London, 1981)

Whitworth Art Gallery, University of Manchester, *British Sources of Art Nouveau* (exhib. cat., Manchester, 1969)

I am grateful to both the Victoria and Albert Museum and Thames & Hudson for making it possible for me to write and select images for this book, and for another excuse (if any is needed) for me to spend time with the extraordinary Victoria and Albert Museum collections and studying this particular aspect of Voysey's design work. Thank you in particular to Hannah Newell and Coralie Hepburn of V&A Publishing for their skilful management and support, to Katy Carter for her thoughtful editing and Isabel Roldan for her book design.

There is always more to discover in the collections and archives, and I very much appreciate the time and support of the people who have facilitated my research. Fiona Orsini is always tremendously friendly and helpful in giving me access to the archives and collections held by the RIBA, and in helping to track down particular images, for which I am very grateful. I should also like to thank Wendy Hitchmough, Tony Peart and Peter King, secretary of the Voysey Society (www.voyseysociety.org), who have all been generous with time and help in answering my queries. Sincere thanks also go to Dru Muskovin and the team at Crab Tree Farm for support and access to the wonderful collections there and for providing images for this book.

Last but not least, this book is for Jonathan and Cordelia, who also love birds and animals.

Karen Livingstone is Director of Masterplan and Estate at the Science Museum, London, and a former curator at the Victoria and Albert Museum. Her previous publications include *C.F.A. Voysey: Arts and Crafts Designer* (with Max Donnelly and Linda Parry) and *Essential Arts and Crafts*.

Cover image: Detail from design for a textile or wallpaper, 1926 (p. 55)
Opposite title page: Design for a wallpaper, 1929 (p. 113)
Opposite contents page: Design for a wallpaper, for Jeffrey & Co., *c.*1900 (p. 63)

First published in the United Kingdom in 2020
by Thames & Hudson Ltd, in association with the
Victoria and Albert Museum, London.

Voysey's Birds and Animals
© 2020 Victoria and Albert Museum, London/Thames & Hudson Ltd, London

Text and V&A photographs © 2020 Victoria and Albert Museum, London
Design © 2020 Thames & Hudson Ltd, London

British Library Cataloguing-in-Publication Data
A catalogue record for this book is available from the British Library

ISBN 978-0-500-48060-1
Printed and bound in China by C&C Offset Printing Co. Ltd

To find out about all our publications, please visit
www.thamesandhudson.com. There you can subscribe to
our e-newsletter, browse or download our current catalogue,
and buy any titles that are in print.

V&A Publishing
Supporting the world's leading
museum of art and design,
the Victoria and Albert
Museum, London